DEREK P

THE Divine Exchange

DPM

Derek Prince Ministries-UK
Baldock, Herfordshire

The Divine Exchange

Published by: DPM–UK, Kingsfield, Hadrian Way, Baldock, SG7 6AN.

UK Edition 2004

ISBN 1-901144-01-1

Printed in the United Kingdom by Creative Print and Design, Harmondsworth Middlesex.

1 2 3 4 5 6 7 8 9 10 / 07 06 05 04

Derek Prince Ministries
http://www.dpmuk.org

An Invitation

Jesus Christ has given an invitation that extends to the whole human race: "Come to me, all you who are weary and burdened, and I will give you rest." No matter what may be your special burden or need or problem, God has an answer for you.

But there is only one place that you can find the answer: the Cross on which Jesus died. It is through the Cross – and the Cross alone – that you may receive the supply of your need, the answer to your problem, the release from your burden.

Read the following pages expectantly!

The Divine Exchange

The entire message of the Gospel revolves around one unique historical event: the sacrificial death of Jesus on the Cross. Concerning this the writer of Hebrews says: "For by one offering [sacrifice] He [Jesus] has perfected forever those who are being sanctified" (Hebrews 10:14). Two powerful expressions are combined: 'perfected' and 'forever.' Together, they depict a sacrifice which comprehends every need of the entire human race. Furthermore, its effects extend throughout time and on into eternity.

It is on the basis of this sacrifice that Paul writes in Philippians 4:19: "And my God shall supply *all your need* according to His riches in glory *by Christ Jesus.*" *All your need* covers every area of your life – your body, your soul, your mind, your emotions, as well as your material and financial needs. Nothing is either so large or so small that it is excluded from God's provision. By a single, sovereign act, God brought together all the need and all the suffering of humanity in one climactic moment of time.

God has not provided many different solutions for the multitudinous problems of mankind. Instead, He offers us one all-sufficient solution which is His answer to every problem. We may come from many different backgrounds, each of us burdened with our own special need, but to receive God's solution we must all make our way to the same place – the Cross of Jesus.

The most complete account of what was accomplished at the Cross was given through the prophet Isaiah, 700 years before it actually took place. In Isaiah 53:10 the prophet depicts a 'servant of the Lord' whose soul was to be offered to God as a sin offering. The writers of the New Testament are unanimous in identifying this unnamed 'servant' as Jesus. The divine purpose accomplished by His sacrifice is summed up in Isaiah 53:6:

> *All we like sheep have gone astray;*
>   *We have turned, every one, to his own way;*
> *And the Lord has laid on Him*
>   *the iniquity of us all.*

Here is the basic, universal problem of all humanity: we have turned, each of us, to our own way. There are various specific sins that many of us have never committed, such as murder, adultery, theft, and so on. But this one thing we all have in common: we have turned to our own way. In so doing, *we have turned our backs on God.* The Hebrew word that sums this up is *avon*, here translated 'iniquity.' Perhaps the closest equivalent in contemporary English would be 'rebellion', not against man, but against God.

However, no one English word, whether it is 'iniquity' or 'rebellion' conveys the full meaning of *avon*. In its biblical use, *avon* describes not merely iniquity but also the punishment, or the evil consequences, that iniquity brings in its train.

For instance, in Genesis 4:13, after God had pronounced judgement on Cain for the murder of his brother, Cain said: "My punishment is greater than I can bear." The word here translated 'punishment' is *avon.* It covered not merely Cain's 'iniquity,' but also the 'punishment' it brought upon him.

In Leviticus 16:22, concerning the scapegoat released on the Day of Atonement, the Lord said: "The goat shall bear on itself all their iniquities to an uninhabited land . . ." In this symbolism, the goat bore not merely the iniquities of the Israelites, but also all the consequences of their iniquities.

In Lamentations 4 *avon* occurs twice with the same meaning. In verse 6 it is translated: "The *punishment of the iniquity* of the daughter of my people . . ." Again, in verse 22: "The *punishment of your iniquity* . . . O daughter of Zion . . ." In each case, the single word *avon* is translated by a complete phrase "the punishment of iniquity." In other words, in its fullest sense *avon* means not simply 'iniquity,' but also includes *all the evil consequences* which God's judgement brings upon iniquity.

This applies to the sacrifice of Jesus on the Cross. Jesus Himself was not guilty of any sin. In Isaiah 53:9 the prophet says, "He had done no violence, nor was any deceit in His mouth." But in verse 6 he says, "the LORD has laid on Him the iniquity [avon] of us all." Not merely was Jesus identified with our iniquity. He also endured all the evil consequences of that iniquity. Like the scapegoat that had prefigured Him, He carried them away, so that they might never return again upon us.

Here is the true meaning and purpose of the Cross. On it a divinely ordained exchange took place. First, Jesus endured in our place all the evil consequences that were due by divine justice to our iniquity. Now, in exchange, God offers us all the good that was due to the sinless obedience of Jesus.

Stated more briefly, the evil due to us came upon Jesus, that, in return, the good due to Jesus might be offered to us. God is able to offer this to us without compromising His own eternal justice, because Jesus has already endured on our behalf all the just punishment due to our iniquities.

All of this proceeds solely out of the unfathomable grace of God, and it is received solely by faith. There is no logical explanation in terms of cause and effect. None of us has ever done anything to deserve such an offer, and none of us can ever do anything to earn it.

Scripture reveals many different aspects of the exchange, and many different areas in which it applies. In each case, however, the same principle holds good:

> *the evil came upon Jesus*
> *that the corresponding good might be*
> *offered to us.*

The first two aspects of the exchange are revealed in Isaiah 53:4-5:

Surely He has borne our griefs [literally, sicknesses]
 And carried our sorrows [literally, pains];
Yet we esteemed Him stricken,
 Smitten by God, and afflicted.
But He was wounded for our transgressions,
 He was bruised for our iniquities;
The chastisement [punishment] for our peace was upon Him,
 And by His stripes [wounds] we are healed.

Two truths are here interwoven, the application of one is spiritual, and of the other is physical. On the spiritual plane, Jesus received the punishment due to our transgressions and iniquities that we, in turn, might be forgiven and so have peace with God. (See Romans 5:1.) On the physical plane, Jesus bore our sicknesses and pains that we through His wounds might be healed.

The physical application of the exchange is confirmed in two passages of the New Testament. Matthew 8:16-17 refers back to Isaiah 53:4 and records that Jesus:

. . . healed all who were sick, that it might be fulfilled which was spoken by Isaiah the prophet, saying:
 "He Himself took our infirmities
  And bore our sicknesses."

Again, in 1 Peter 2:24, the apostle refers back to Isaiah 53:5-6 and says of Jesus:

. . . who Himself bore our sins in His own body on the tree, that we, having died to sins, might live for righteousness – by whose stripes [wounds] you were healed.

The twofold exchange described in the above verses may be summed up as follows:

Jesus was punished
 that we might be forgiven.

Jesus was wounded
 that we might be healed.

A third aspect of the exchange is revealed in Isaiah 53:10, which states that the Lord made the soul of Jesus 'an offering for sin.' This must be understood in the light of the Mosaic ordinances for various forms of sin offering. The person who had sinned was required to bring his sacrificial offering – a sheep, a goat, a bull, or some other animal, to the priest. He would confess his sin over the offering, and the priest would symbolically transfer the sin he had confessed from the person to the animal. Then the animal would be killed, thus paying the penalty for the sin that had been transferred to it.

In the foreknowledge of God, all this was designed to foreshadow what was to be accomplished by the final, all-sufficient sacrifice of Jesus. On the Cross, the sin of the whole world was transferred to the soul of Jesus. The outcome is described in Isaiah 53:12: "He poured out His soul unto death." By His sacrificial, substitutionary death, Jesus made atonement for the sin of the whole human race.

In 2 Corinthians 5:21 Paul refers to Isaiah 53:10 and, at the same time, he also presents the positive aspect of the exchange:

For He [God] made Him [Jesus] who knew no sin to be sin for us,
that we might become the righteousness of God in Him.

Paul does not speak here about any kind of righteousness that we can achieve by our own efforts, but about God's own righteousness – a righteousness that has never known sin. None of us can ever earn this. It is as high above our own righteousness as heaven is above earth. It can be received solely by faith.

This third aspect of the exchange may be summed up as follows:

Jesus was made sin with our sinfulness
   that we might be made righteous
   with His righteousness.

The next aspect of the exchange is a logical outworking of the previous one. The entire Bible, in both the Old Testament and the New, emphasises that the final outcome of sin is death. In Ezekiel 18:4 the Lord states, "The soul who sins shall die." In James 1:15 the apostle says, "sin, when it is full-grown, brings forth death." When Jesus became identified with our sin, it was inevitable that He should also experience the death which is the outcome of sin.

In confirmation of this, in Hebrews 2:9, the writer says that "Jesus . . . was made a little lower than the angels, for the suffering of death . . . that He, by the grace of God, might taste death for everyone." The death that He died was the inevitable outcome of human sin which he had taken upon Himself. He bore the sin of all men, and so died the death due to all men.

In return, to all who accept His substitutionary sacrifice, Jesus now offers the gift of eternal life. In Romans 6:23 Paul sets the two alternatives side by side:

For the wages [just reward] of sin is death, but the [unearned] gift of God is eternal life in Christ Jesus our Lord.

Thus the fourth aspect of the exchange may be summed up as follows:

Jesus died our death
   that we might receive His life.

A further aspect of the exchange is stated by Paul in 2 Corinthians 8:9:

For you know the grace of our Lord Jesus Christ, that though He was rich, yet for your sakes He became poor, that you through His poverty might become rich.

The exchange is clear: from poverty to riches. Jesus became poor that we in return might become rich.

When did Jesus become poor? Some people picture Him as poor throughout His earthly ministry, but this is not accurate. He Himself did not carry a lot of cash, but at no time did He lack anything He needed. When He sent His disciples out on their own, they likewise lacked nothing. (See Luke 22:35.) So, far from being poor, He and His disciples made a regular practice of giving to the poor. (See John 12:4-8; 13:29.)

True, Jesus' methods of obtaining money were sometimes unconventional, but money has the same value, whether withdrawn from a bank or the mouth of a fish! (See Matthew 17:27.) His methods of providing food were also at times unconventional, but a man who can provide a

10

substantial meal for 5,000 men (plus women and children) certainly would not be considered poor by normal standards! (See Matthew 14:15-21)

Actually, throughout His earthly ministry, Jesus exactly exemplified 'abundance,' as defined in the Bible. He always had all that He needed to do the will of God in His own life. Over and above this, He was continually giving out to others, and His supply was never exhausted.

So when did Jesus become poor for our sakes? The answer is: *on the Cross.* In Deuteronomy 28:48 Moses summed up absolute poverty in four expressions: hunger, thirst, nakedness, and need of all things. Jesus experienced all this in its fullness on the Cross.

He was *hungry.* He had not eaten for nearly 24 hours.

He was *thirsty.* One of His last utterances was: 'I thirst!' (John 19:28).

He was *naked.* The soldiers had taken all His clothes from Him (John 19:23).

He was *in need of all things.* He no longer owned anything whatever. After His death He was buried in a borrowed robe and in a borrowed tomb (Luke 23:50-53). Thus, Jesus, exactly and completely, endured *absolute poverty* for our sakes.

In 2 Corinthians 9:8 Paul presents more fully the positive side of the exchange:

And God is able to make all grace abound toward you, that you, always having all sufficiency in all things, have an abundance for every good work.

Paul is careful to emphasise throughout that the only basis for this exchange is God's grace. It can never be earned. It can only be received by faith.

Very often our 'abundance' will be like that of Jesus while He was on earth. We shall not carry large amounts of cash, or have large deposits in a bank. But from day to day we shall have enough for our own needs, and something over for the needs of others.

One important reason for this level of provision is indicated by the words of Jesus quoted in Acts 20:35: "It is more blessed to give than to receive." God's purpose is that all His children should be able to enjoy the greater blessing. Therefore, He provides us with enough to cover our own needs and also to give to others.

This fifth aspect of the exchange may be summed up:

Jesus endured our poverty
that we might share His abundance.

The exchange at the Cross covers also the emotional forms of suffering that follow from man's iniquity. Here again, Jesus endured the evil that we in turn might enjoy the good. Two of the most cruel wounds brought upon us by our iniquity are *shame* and *rejection*. Both these came upon Jesus on the Cross.

Shame can vary in intensity from acute embarrassment to a cringing sense of unworthiness that cuts a person off from meaningful fellowship either with God or with man. One of the commonest causes – becoming more and more prevalent in our contemporary society – is some form of sexual abuse or molestation in childhood. Often this leaves scars that can only be healed by the grace of God.

Speaking of Jesus on the Cross, the writer of Hebrews says that He "endured the Cross, *despising the shame* . . . " (Hebrews 12:2). Execution on a Cross was the most shameful of all forms of death, reserved for the lowest class of criminal. The person to be executed was stripped of all his clothing and exposed naked to the gaze of passers-by, who jeered and mocked. This was the degree of shame which Jesus endured as He hung on the Cross (Matthew 27:35-44).

In place of the shame which Jesus bore, God's purpose is to bring those who trust in Him to share His eternal glory. In Hebrews 2:10 the writer says:

For it was fitting for Him (God) . . . in bringing many sons to glory,
to make the author of their salvation [that is, Jesus] perfect through
sufferings.

The shame which Jesus endured on the Cross has opened the way for all who trust in Him to be released from their own shame. Not only that, but He then shares with us the glory which belongs to Him by eternal right!

There is another wound which is often even more agonising than shame. It is *rejection*. Usually this stems from some form of broken relationship. In its earliest form, it is caused by parents who reject their own children. The rejection may be active, expressed in harsh, negative ways; or it may be merely a failure to show love and acceptance. If a pregnant woman entertains negative feelings toward the infant in her womb, the child will probably be born with a sense of rejection, which may continue into adulthood, and even to the grave.

The breakup of a marriage is another frequent cause of rejection. This is vividly pictured in the words of the Lord in Isaiah 54:6:

"The Lord will call you back
    as if you were a wife deserted and distressed in spirit –
a wife who married young,
    only to be rejected," says your God.   (NIV)

God's provision for healing the wound of rejection is recorded in Matthew 27:46 and 50, which describe the culmination of the agony of Jesus:

And about the ninth hour Jesus cried out with a loud voice, saying, "Eli, Eli, lama sabachthani?" that is, "My God, My God, why have You forsaken Me?"
Jesus, when He had cried out again with a loud voice, yielded up His spirit.

For the first time in the history of the universe, the Son of God called out to His Father and received no response. So fully was Jesus identified with man's iniquity that the uncompromising holiness of God caused Him to reject even His own Son. In this way Jesus endured rejection in its most agonising form: rejection by a father. Almost immediately after that, He died, not of the wounds of crucifixion, but of a heart broken by rejection.

The record of Matthew continues immediately: "And behold, the veil of the temple was torn in two from top to bottom . . ." Symbolically this demonstrated that the way had been opened for sinful man to enter into direct fellowship with a holy God. The rejection of Jesus had opened the way for us to be accepted by God as His children. This is summed up by Paul in Ephesians 1:5-6:

> *"having predestined us to adoption as sons by Jesus Christ to Himself . . . He [God] has made us accepted in the Beloved"* (KJV)

The rejection of Jesus resulted in our acceptance.

God's remedy for shame and rejection has never been more desperately needed than it is today. My estimate is that at least one-quarter of the adults in the world today suffer from wounds of shame or rejection. It has given me measureless joy to point such people to the healing that flows from the Cross of Jesus.

The two emotional aspects of the exchange at the Cross that have been analysed above may be summarised as follows:

Jesus bore our shame
 that we might share His glory.

Jesus endured our rejection
 that we might have His acceptance
 with the Father

The aspects of the exchange analysed above cover some of humanity's most basic and urgent needs, but they are by no means exhaustive. Actually, there is no need resulting from man's rebellion that is not covered by the same principle of exchange: the evil came upon Jesus that the good might be offered to us. Once we have learned to apply this principle in our lives, it releases God's provision for every need.

There remains one final, climactic aspect of the exchange, described by Paul in Galatians 3:13-14:

Christ has redeemed us from the curse of the law, having become a curse for us (for it is written, "Cursed is everyone who hangs on a tree"), that the blessing of Abraham might come upon the Gentiles in Christ Jesus, that we might receive the promise of the Spirit through faith.

Paul applies to Jesus on the Cross an enactment of the law of Moses, stated in Deuteronomy 21:23, according to which a person executed by hanging on a 'tree' (a wooden gibbet) thereby came under the curse of God. Then he points to the resulting opposite: the blessing.

It does not require a theologian to analyse this aspect of the exchange:

**Jesus became a curse
that we might enter into the blessing.**

The curse that came upon Jesus is defined as "the curse of the law." In Deuteronomy 28, Moses gives an exhaustive list of both the blessings that result from obeying the law and the curses that result from breaking it. The curses listed in Deuteronomy 28:15-68 may be summed up as follows:

- *Humiliation*
- *Barrenness, unfruitfulness*
- *Mental and physical sickness*
- *Family breakdown*
- *Poverty*
- *Defeat*
- *Oppression*
- *Failure*
- *God's disfavour*

Do some of these words apply to areas in your life? Are there things that rest like a dark shadow over you, shutting out the sunlight of God's blessing that you long for? If so, it may well be that the root cause of your problems is a curse, from which you need to be released.

To appreciate the full horror of the curse that came upon Jesus, try to picture Him as He hung there on the Cross.

Jesus had been rejected by His own countrymen, betrayed by one of His disciples, and abandoned by the rest (though some later returned to follow His final agony). He was suspended naked between earth and heaven. His body was wracked by the pain of innumerable wounds, His soul weighed down by the guilt of all humanity. Earth had rejected Him, and heaven would not respond to His cry. As the sun withdrew its light and darkness covered Him, His life blood ebbed out onto the dusty, stony soil. Yet out of the darkness, just before He expired, there came one final, triumphant cry: "It is finished!"

In the Greek text that phrase, "It is finished," consists of only one word. It is the perfect tense of a verb that means 'to make something complete or perfect.' In English, it could be rendered: 'It is completely complete' or 'It is perfectly perfect.'

Jesus had taken upon Himself every evil consequence that rebellion had brought upon humanity. He had exhausted every curse of God's broken law. All this, that we in turn might receive every blessing due to His obedience. Such a sacrifice is stupendous in its scope, yet marvellous in its simplicity.

Have you been able to accept with faith this account of the sacrifice of Jesus and of all that He has obtained for you? Are you now eager to enter into God's full provision?

There is one barrier that we must all deal with, the barrier of unforgiven sin. Do you already have a clear assurance that your sins have been forgiven because of the sacrifice of Jesus? If not, that is where you must begin.

You can offer just a simple prayer:

God, I acknowledge that I am a sinner and there is unforgiven sin in my life. But I believe that Jesus was punished that I might be forgiven, and so I ask you now; Forgive all my sins, in Jesus' name.

God's Word promises that "if we confess our sins, He is faithful and just to forgive us our sins and to cleanse us from all unrighteousness"

(1 John 1:9). Take God at His word! This very moment believe that He has indeed forgiven you for all your sins!

16

There is one simple response that you need to make, a response which is the simplest and purest expression of true faith. It is to say "Thank you!"

Do that right now! Say, "Thank you! Thank you, Lord Jesus, that you were punished that I might be forgiven. I do not fully understand, but I do believe and I am grateful!"

With the barrier of sin removed, the way is open for you to enter into all the other provisions God has made through the Cross. Just like the forgiveness of sin, each must be received by simple faith in God's Word.

Each of us has special needs and each of us must come to God individually to accept His provision. Here is a general form of words that you may use to claim any of the other provisions described in this booklet.

Lord Jesus, I thank you that you were wounded
    that I might be healed.

Lord Jesus, I thank you that you were made sin with my sinfulness
    that I might be made righteous with your righteousness.

Lord Jesus, I thank you that you died my death
    that I might receive your life.

Lord Jesus, I thank you that you endured my poverty
    that I might share your abundance.

Lord Jesus, I thank you that you bore my shame
    that I might share your glory.

Lord Jesus, I thank you that you suffered my rejection
    that I might have your acceptance with the Father.

Lord Jesus, I thank you that you were made a curse
    that I might enter into the blessing.

Each provision you have prayed for is progressive. Your initial prayer has released God's power into your life. However, that is merely the starting point. In order to appropriate the full provision that you are seeking, you will need to do three things:

1. Search out these truths for yourself in the Bible.

2. Continually reaffirm the particular aspect of the exchange which answers to your need.

3. Continually reaffirm your faith by thanking God for what He has provided.

The more you thank God, the more you will believe what He has done for you. And the more you believe, the more you will want to thank Him.

These two things – believing and thanking, thanking and believing, are like a spiral staircase that will take you continually higher into the fullness of God's provision.

The Exchange
Made at the Cross

There is one, and only one all-sufficient basis for every provision of God's mercy: the exchange that took place on the Cross.

Jesus was punished
that we might be forgiven.

Jesus was wounded
that we might be healed.

Jesus was made sin with our sinfulness
that we might be made righteous with His righteousness.

Jesus died our death
that we might receive His life.

Jesus endured our poverty
that we might share His abundance.

Jesus bore our shame
that we might share His glory

Jesus endured our rejection
that we might have His acceptance with the Father.

Jesus was made a curse
that we might enter into the blessing.

This list is not complete. There are other aspects of the exchange that could be added. But all of them are different facets of the provision which God has made through the sacrifice of Jesus. The Bible sums them up in one grand, all-inclusive word: *salvation.* Christians often limit salvation to the experience of having one's sins forgiven and being born again. Wonderful though this is, however, it is only the first part of the total salvation revealed in the New Testament.

UNLOCK THE TREASURES OF GOD'S PROVISION

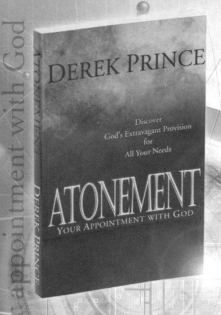

ATONEMENT: Your appointment with God

If you have enjoyed this book and want to explore the subject further,

ATONEMENT: YOUR APPOINTMENT WITH GOD

is the next book for you. This thorough study, 224 pages long, examines how we can appropriate the provisions of the atonement for all our needs.

'Through the sacrifice of Jesus on the Cross, an exchange took place that unlocks all the treasures of God's provision.'

ISBN: 1-901144-19-4

Pages: 224

Price £8.99

Available from your local Christian bookshop or Derek Prince Ministries – UK

Kingsfield • Hadrian Way • Baldock • SG7 6AN

Tel:+(0)44 1462 492100 • www.dpmshop.org

BUILDING ON GOD'S WORD

with Derek Prince Ministries

War in Heaven
1-901144-23-2 £6.99

If evil was defeated at the Cross, why does it
continue to exist?

How are we to await the end of the age?

They Shall Expel Demons
1-901144-06-2 £7.99

'Twenty years ago I was so demonised
that there was no hope for me. Then I
met Jesus and somebody gave me
your tape on deliverance.
Now I'm free!'

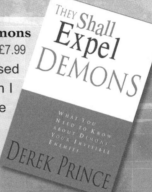

Foundations For Christian Living
1-901144-25-9 £9.99

When times are difficult, you need to stand firm in
your faith. This indispensable book gives you
everything you need to develop a strong,
balanced, Spirit-filled life.

DPM

BUILDING ON GOD'S WORD

with Derek Prince Ministries

Blessing or Curse: You Can Choose!
1-901144-02-X £7.99

'The main vehicle of both blessings and curses is words . . . find out how the devil has been deceiving and cheating us.'

Thanksgiving, Praise and Worship
1-901144-03-8 £5.95

'Don't focus on your feelings. Don't focus on your situation. Focus on these eternal, unchanging aspects of God's nature and of His dealings with us. Then you will find yourself thanking God ceaselessly.'

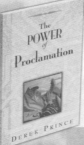

The Power of Proclamation
1-901144-22-4 £5.99

Be ready! The book to use as a tool for proclaiming God's Word in every circumstance.

Sound Judgement
1-901144-21-6 £5.95

Discernment in judging is a prayer on many believer's lips in these 'end times'. Derek offers sound and effective principles to help you walk righteously before God.